<u>I Am, Am I Not Me…., At All ?</u>

I am
Behold Me I'd love to daresay
The One and only, I once used to say

Then I saw, this other face
Akin mine, yet alien so, in every which way

That, seemed well able, to twist and tort me
In all and every, of my way and say

I knew then as true,
And, to this day

That, as much
I'd yearn to hold real sway

This Other,
This Lucifer, always, can have own say

The trespass of so many eons in past,
Still cloaks strong in evil grasp

The once wispy winsome ways
Are now heavy on me, despite my wizened greys

I have now learned, that I am the One
But, am, ever seen as this other scrooge

That the only hope for the real Me
To reckon wise, quell the alien deep within

That I may soon, be able
Again, to come up smiling, say
As the sole and only

At final call, daresay…
Yes
I am

Or, atleast, whence all be done and I begone
The World shalt, in relent, say mayhaps…..
Yes, I was

(Not, after all said and done, A mere <May have been> after all !

Through the embrace of Life in all its manifest, I too have had my ample share of internal duels with that foul alien, the other one within.

Innumerable are the milestones strewn along the way, each, a memorial to unequal duels of duality within.

Each, vying with the other; and, so oft, the valiant made to stand down meek in the turn of events; and, the vile ones getting away with their spoils ill wrought.

So many Tsunamis, big and small, each one a back stabbing killer, each time, so faced, endured, won upon! And, in duress if, yet survived each one, every time; and, today still standing as tall…..

Such wins could only have become possible, solely and primarily, only due to the presence of so many Guardian Angel manifesting in human form, to help us through and reach us our target destined goals..

And, as so, have I been blessed with my Angels too; who, time and again, have stood by, alongside and reached down to pick me upon; and set me forth, post any and all of my trips and falls.

I bow my head, torso and spirit afore all of you, my angels in life, who remained steadfast in believing there indeed was the God-invested, truer form of me, vesting deep within, a resilient inner self, than what other mortal eyes could see; and having sought; merely deeming to stalk unforgivingly and pith duly stain.

To all ye, who deemed it wise and fit to pull me up again and push me through the dark tunnels of vile; and see the light again, I offer my humble prostrations and this tale, in
even humbler tribute.

Keitiekei

Table of Contents

1. **Cover**
2. **Preface**
3. **I Am, Am I Not Me…… At All?**
4. **Acknowledgement**
5. **Index**

6. **<u>Section 1 - In The Beginning.</u>**
   - Pure Bliss, The Perennial Exist
   - Cosmic Unfurl, In All New Play
   - Change- Imminent, Persistent, Permanent

7. **<u>Section 2 - The Arrival from Twilight Zone</u>**
   - Weaned to the Womb Pg 1 of 2
   - Weaned to the Womb Pg 2 of 2

8. **<u>Section 3 - An Entity Sculpted</u>**
   - Learning the "I" Cry
   - Bright Days, Lit Up Nights

9. **<u>Section 4 - Nestled Bliss</u>**
   - Childhood Steer, In Warm Gear Pg 1 of 2
   - Childhood Steer, In Warm Gear Pg 2 of 2

10. **<u>Section 5 - Rise Of The Fledgeling</u>**
    - Nest O'Fun, To Wind & Sun
    - Learning to Fend, Tend, Contend

11. **<u>Section 6 - Treading Every New Path, Strong, Steadfast</u>**
    - Mile-stoned Paths, Life Travails
12. **<u>Section 7 - At Final Goal Post</u>**
    - Rendezvous Done, Pack Shack, Adieu - Pg 1 of 2
    - Rendezvous Done, Pack Shack, Adieu - Pg 2 of 2

13. **Final Word –Keitiekei**
14. **Back Cover**

Section 1 : In the Beginning

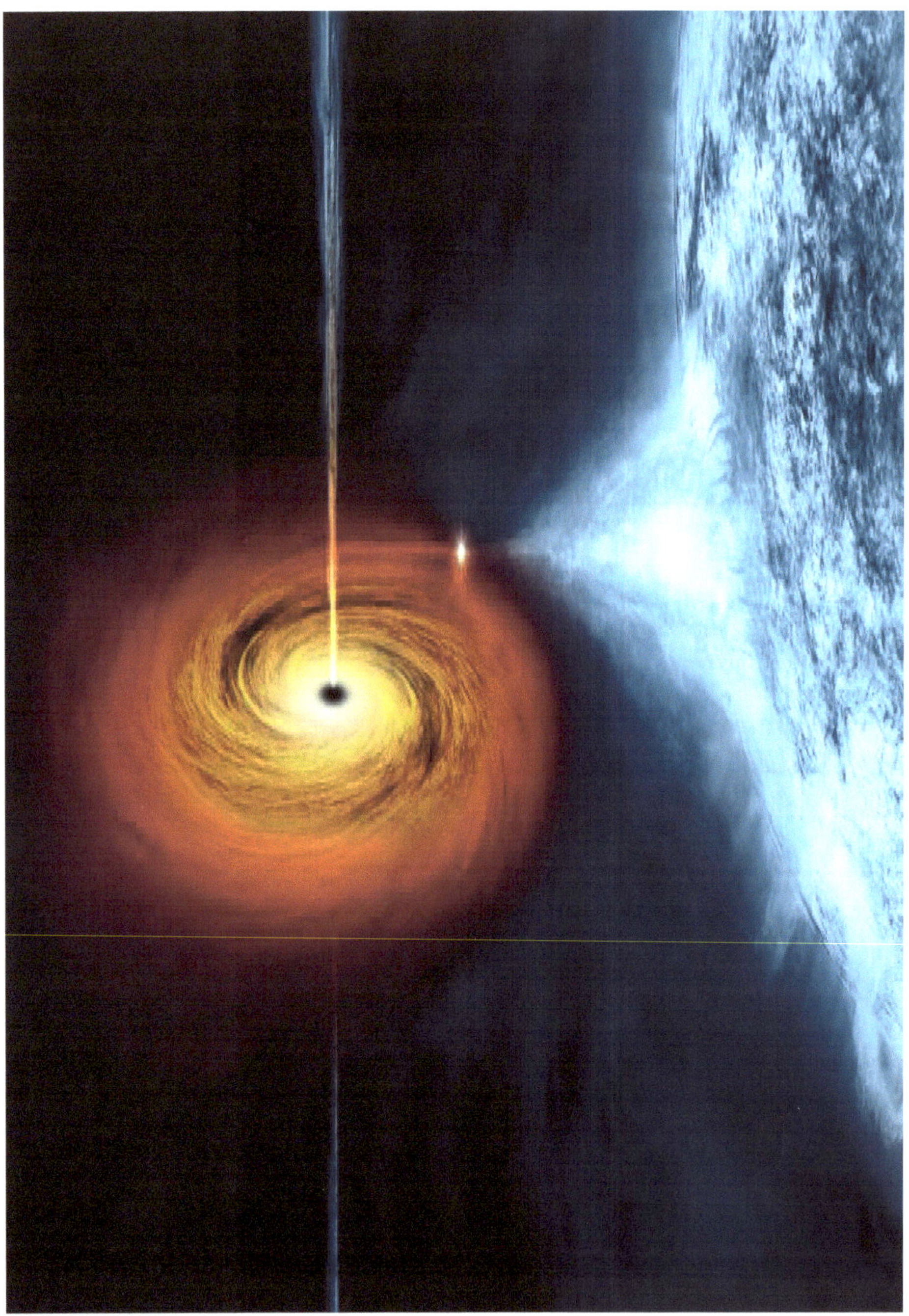

**From The Sanctity Of The Whole
An "I" Pulled -To Play Out A Finite
Yet Undefined Role**

Pure Bliss, The Perennial Exist

Gentle float all around
Unknown to the mortal mind
There is the sea of bliss
With neither start nor finish.
Pure, Complete

No push, no jostle
No pangs, no scams
No worry, no pretence
No sound, no noise
No dark, no light

No aches, no pains
No yours, no mine
No future, no past,
No present

Pure omnipresent
No qualms, no fears
No greed, no games
No thirst, no hunger
No need, no desire
Only the perennial,
Eternal hum
Ceaseless
Formless
Bondless
Pure, set

Beyond
Known, Unknown
Light, Dark
Limits Of
Moral, immoral
Mortal mind

The "I" unborn
In total union
Fully within
The one and only
Whole

Cosmic Unfurl, In All New Play

T'was as if
Like a huge yawn from deep slumber
Still no sound, Yet, there was
This gentle nudge as if, something,
Somewhere, new, about to start

As if
The colossal depth of the celestial dark
Wanted now to move from a bliss of still
To some new rhyme, some new rhythm
With all its grace intact, was now keen
For a new cosmic song, a dance to star

As if
Some Master had moved his little finger
Wanting to nudge from prevailing hush
The silent cosmos into awakening task
Wondering mayhaps, to see the cosmos
In fuller glory, change from its still, so stark?

As if
Someone watching over, loving what was,
Wanted just to pry, to probe, to play a bit,
Would the bliss sustain, if made to move
From still?

And, as if,
In equal sequence, from this nascent thought,
Came the first budge, arising from this nudge,
Shimmering, shivering, almost too shy at first,

There came the gentle move of pulse it seemed
The cosmic, in keen response, undulating gently
Commenced its sway to new rhyme and rhythm
Coming its way.

And, as if,
One gentle ripple putting full pond to play
A Celestial Dance so begun, indeed, here to stay
In that very opportune moment when all o' the still
Made way for the new swerve and gay and frills

For, within the earlier, Unified One,
An "I" became born;
And this entity in duality was also
As if, in one form or another,
Was forever, here, to stay.

Change- Imminent, Persistent, Permanent

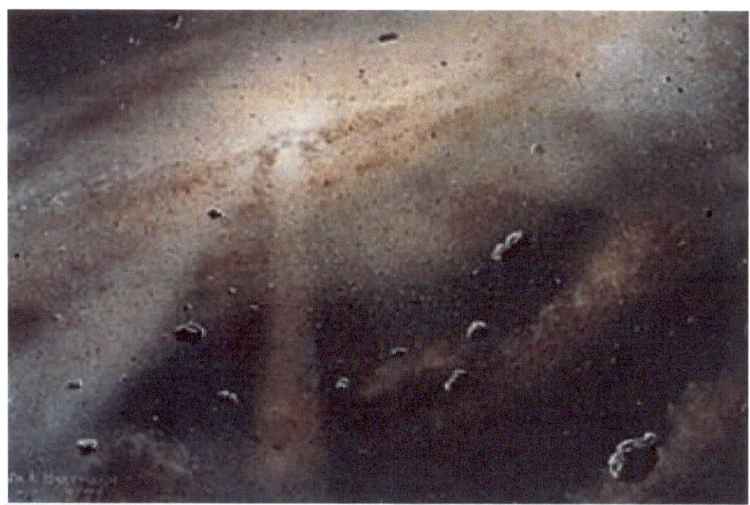

Born of a thought, a flicker of sorts,
That moment in time, as it swerved
Its first movement from still stock
Change had made its will upon all

Hereon, no matter what,
The ones pulled in cosmic consort
Would serve ever,
To this Master's writ and wrath

None would have power of way
As change would oft, make its say
From state of bliss to cosmic sway
Each, now puppet, its perennial play

And yet
These parts, being an ultimate Whole
There seemed to be an ultimate goal
For all to strive through trysts of change
Someday, to become still and firm
Be that part of the Whole again

And, each to rise to the call of play
Was bestowed a mind in full "I" say
Only rue, would be to note,
This mind would play in dual quote

Alongside "I" and the mind so adorned
Inevitably, its twin too was born
From that moment till end of its time
The perennial duality to persist
Of "I" and its twin, the alien foe

Nary what the mind would say,
Right from wrong was ever at stake
And oft, fully known, only post play
So, with every act, oft comes react
And, with every opt, the duel intact

Whether there be a fork in road or not,
T'is the step we take upon path select,
That we end up in smile or foul brow
The better we team with our true "I"
The faster the alien within, destroyed

That, end of it all, we may, head held high,
Return, to the still Whole, from whence we
Once had come.

Section 2 : The Arrival
 From Twilight Zone

The Journey To Finite Form

<u>Weaned to the Womb</u>

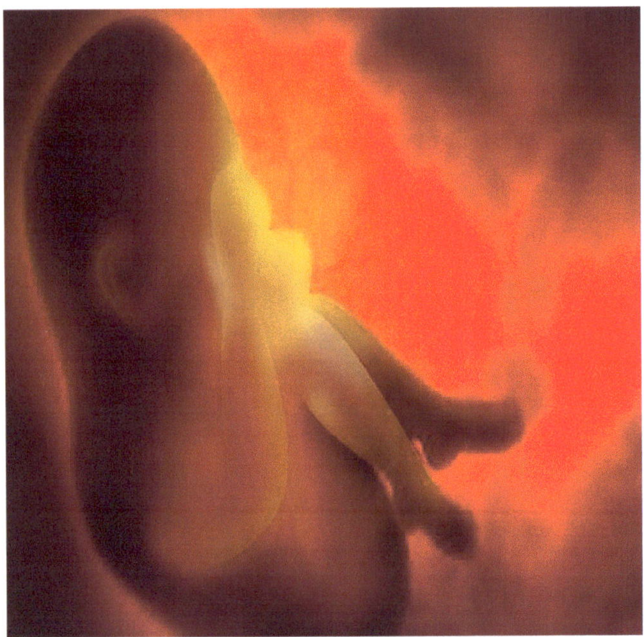

The Nudge, felt at first
The gentle perceive
The slow turn of posture
Then, ere another moment

Moved,
From being with the One
To the microcosmic hold
Of another
Womb

Knowing nought at first
Still not in fathom
Of what it was
That was happening
What it was
That was about to come
In form of becoming
The "I" unborn

The bliss had changed
Now, more and more
Ever changing
Yet, a bliss all the same

There was this knowing
Of being cradled, cared
Inside another,
Home?

A sprout from one to two,
Then, the so many,
In no time, firmed in aspect
New bonding simply happening?

Fears, Feelings, till now unknown
The pitch of dark, an only known
Dull light, sounds, sense of move

At times, sweet caressing notes
At times, gruff yet similar quotes
An all new state of restless rest
An all new feel of give and take

Knowing
If, when, what and how
Was all new comfort zone
The Why, albeit, in crimson zone

Growth of skill
Amass of shape
An all new mind in inner take
Why all this? What next at stake?

A new beat in me within
In sync with the farther beat akin
And, the new give and take
Seemed okay now, to stay this way
Then all sudden, came tumult

Worse than any similar cult
Heaved and shoved beyond it all
Crushed and pushed into a ball?

Nothing the same, pushed to brink
Not one solace giving thought
Nestled bliss, totally lost
Now, enraged, I took the fall

Only to be thrashed black and blue
 As held high, in blinding light,
And all the sudden infernal noise
I too, gave it my vocal hue

This was new, the wailing cry,
So high in note, my fit of wry,
Through handle and fondle
I too, could move

Then, a crooning familiar note
And, a new yet familiar touch
Brought me a sense of peace
At last

Now new born though I was
I knew this as a firm friendly face
For me, For life time, to last

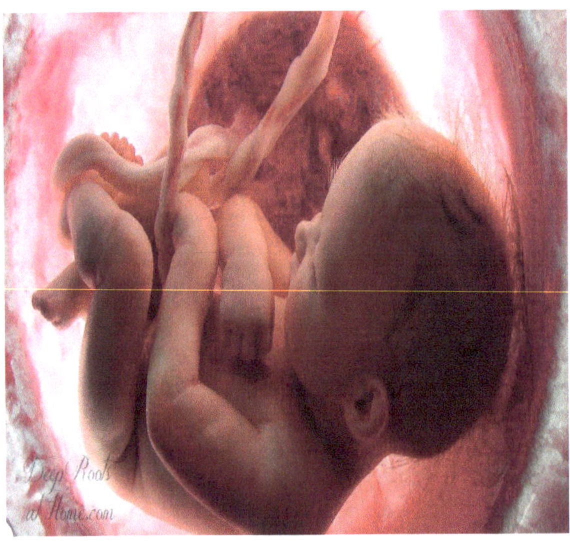

Section 3 :
An Entity Sculpted

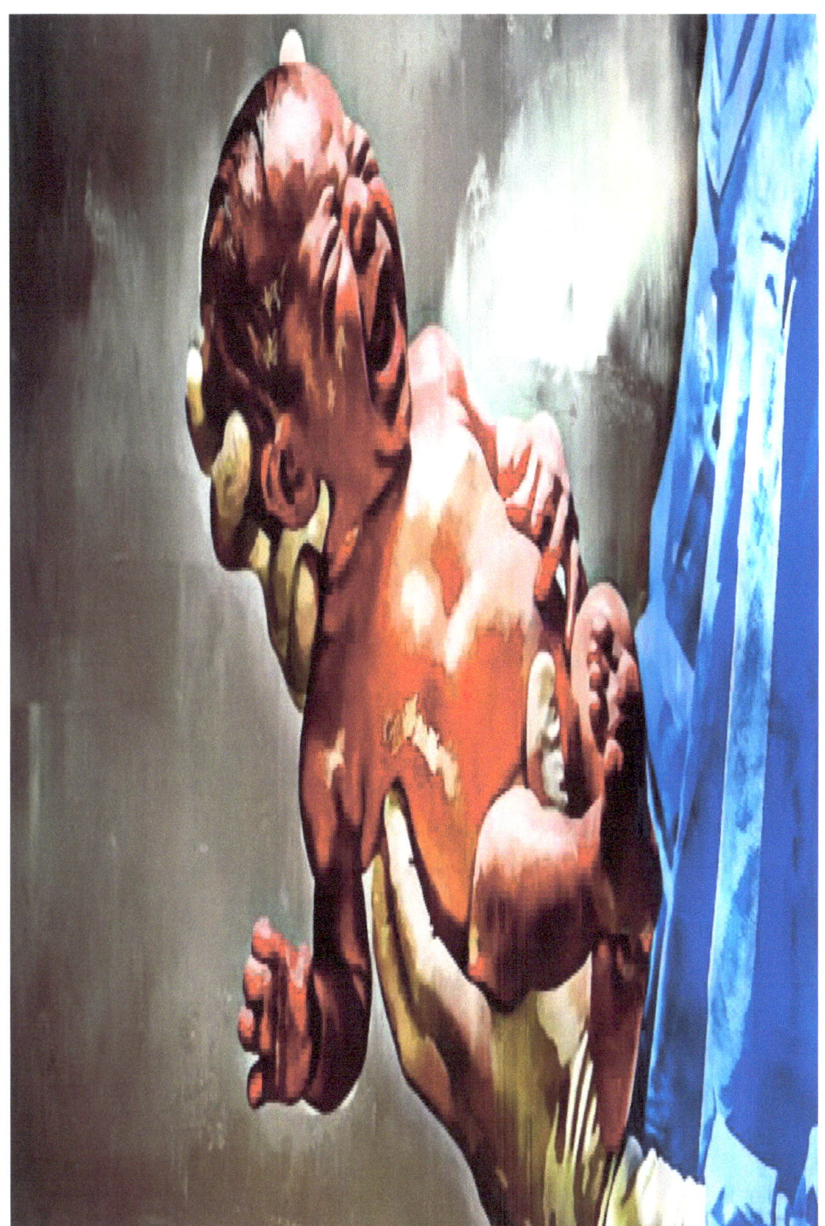

**From The Void of Null
To the Intricacies of "I"**

Learning the "I" Cry

Soon
Grew to see the pattern
Of this new ambient
Of Lights, Sounds and
The hues of change

Soon
Also knew the way
The variants in cascades
Could be dealt with
In my own way

And
Though bound in
Such helpless cloak
Learnt, could muster
Enough clout amongst

So
It came to pass that
I could, on every need,
Beckon, make them till```
Make it work, at my will

 For
Every cry, drew caring hush
Every move, brought love in gush
Every shove, the return nudge
Every gore, cleansed sans grudge

Soon
Could differ the friend from foe
Could filter cries to hoe
Could trust upon the bosom flow
Could reign upon, in nascent glow

Bliss
This was, of another kind
Wuthering whispers

Caressing, kind
Held by hugs I knew were mine

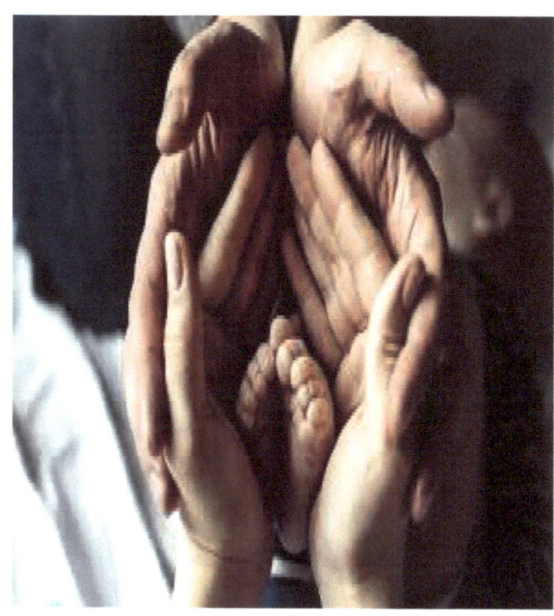

Bright Days, Lit Up Nights

Learning to decipher
Light of day
Lit up night from dark
Love in enact, every play

Dry & soft from wet & grey
Soft Bosom Cuddles from
Hard muscle strength at play

Whispers of mater from
Those of Pater
When & whom to engage
For each want, prank & play

Rhymes, lullaby & cradled songs
From the gruff & growl of male bastion
Akin, yet unique in each content
Learning the hold, in every intent
Soon, learning of work to be done
No more mere laid back summon
Learning to flex & twist & turn
Sit, stand, step, up and run

Every new act, bringing apt applause
Every fall, revived in new effort rigors
Every pause, lifted to fresh new cause
Every step along the way,

Learning to look beyond mortal gait
Life was this, in all its sway
Loving its swing through work & gay,
Light & dark, cousins were entwined strays
And indeed, for me, here to stay

Learning now to deal along
Life was such a wonder song
Lost in act, or, moan loud & long
Life, so firm & finite, was also an infinite song

Section 4 :
Nestled Bliss

**From Cradle O'Womb
To Cradled Bloom**

Childhood Steer, In Warm Gear

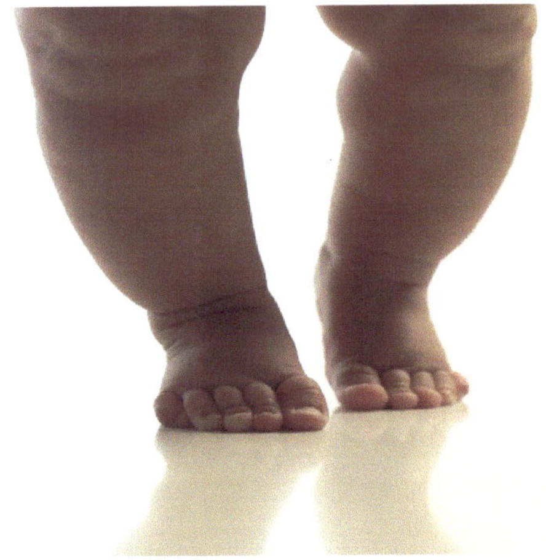

Soon came time
For end of lullabies
And, cradled songs
Cynosure no less
All of love, Still,
At beck & call
Yet

Aware of change
Cradle to toddle
Come asunder
Free of crib
To roam on mat
New twists & turns

Push, pull, lift,
Grab & grope
To claim new spot
It'd be mine
If I claimed my lot
Then, anticipate

Sitting up still,
Applause to
New steering skill
I would have to squat
In an all new cradle o'sorts
Push & roll, across
Pave & block

Having come thus far
More to go, I had to
Learn to take step at will
Then, came the step
To walk, fall, get up
Trod, tumble, run across

Full of glee &bloated pride
I had now become more human
In all my cloned up walk

Walking true, soon came to be
And yet, there was more,
Came the call to take up talk

All earlier spake, soon just stalled
I had now, to make selfish pitch
Scale skills of gab in worldly preach

Ma & Pa, and any in line
Just craved to push and pull
Words from mouth

In place of praise
Came more call to work
Never a moment bereft
Ever placed on center stage

Needs were met
Was saving grace
Though, every moment,
In strife; else, saying grace

What was all this leading to
Where was the next day of
Wandering, leading to
Was all this fun & frolic to be
Was there or,
Worse, pent up in store, for me ?

Life, somehow, seemed to move
Each day anew, new night sinew
Learnt of new rules of the game
No more mere fun and play
Errors were pitfalls, with price to pay

And so, came up my sapien form
From womb to crib cradle & fall
To sit & stand & walk & run
To cope up even, to love lost fares

Home still. was this place of fun
Where, head held high
In naïve childhood steer

And warm hearth of homely gear
Still, to all and sundry,
Numero one

Learning Of New Steps
Yearning Virgin Flights

<u>Nest O'Fun, To Wind & Sun</u>

Feathers are a-sprout,
Strong now, the flap of wings
Endearing though
The nest still is
Even so, time is nigh
To quest new spring
And, whence, the tremors
In limb and swing, stalk
The spirit to remain within,
The writ is done, all writhe to end
Elders all, kith and kin

 Flap to fly bestowing the only win
Are agog so, for some new begin
They nudge & push with their might
Their ward to go forth in altered swing
Cries & pleas to stay within,
Brought to nought,
The new journey begins

Was all fear, this all new steer
Alien faces seen sudden, up close & near
Until, seen, happenings many & similar,
Of domains akin, far and near
Transient clouds, yet skies all clear
Mayhaps, the fledgling felt safer
Letting go of the umbilical hold

Flocking along with new found peers
A first of the many perhaps to come
Drying tears, waning & waxing fear
Be put on hold, to face new frontier
A drop meeting drop,
An ocean in poder
A step and more, in step with another
Soon, the flock in flock, flying together
As the elders, away from them,
And so, will it again come to pass

Remain, in a song of their own
New will soon make way beyond the past
The elders well aware of the die as cast
Staunch in support, yet, learning soon

To let go, step back
When the young wings in glee shall so flap
For, they, in turn, shall now return to nest
And, rest, as the fledglings put life to test

Learning to Fend, Tend, Contend

Life is fun, is best to see, perceive
Though, not always is it so manifest
Can concoct broth of variant taste
Love it or leave it, nary choice to make

For, when It's served, hot or cold
Ain't much left having bit the bait
With the scream or the cream
Learn to spade and wade

Make forward path,
No matter what it takes
Every moment, new learning curve
Life spins for all, but, lasting scores

Learn each day, at Life school
To fend, tend, contend every role
Rise and fall, are cascading waves
Fall or not, look up & rise once again

Passing age, the skills so gained
Fine, refine, gain on pain
And, as we do, life fleets on ahead
Ere we know, our say's been said
We change, as we grow
We reap, as we sow
Choices given and so made
Oft, mere franchise of give and take

The steps, the turns, be the miles we make
We are, in fact, of the choices we make

Section 6 :
Treading Every New Path,
Strong, Steadfast

Daring In Effort
Fight To Last

Milestoned Paths, Life Travails

The milestones all, stand
Stemmed in, as it were,
Oblivious almost, yet,
Obvious in presence so

We may do what we need do
Or, even not do what we can,
Either which way we take a turn
Or, mere stand, sit, gaze, yearn
They stay put, as if, in witness
Of our firm act, taking full toll
Or, our failing to show up at poll

If, in win,
They afford memories fond
They, can add to recall, in abundance,
The woe and rue, of failed determine
T'd be for us, by act and din,
To post our effort and our win

Travails are their comrade cousins,
They muse along our mile-stoned paths,
Through our every r grit & writhe & grin
That every bruise on our shin and skin
The throes of our daily do and din
Thaw in time, to reign our sun & dim our sin

We need to keep our ado up
Do our bit and share our do
Having done it all, then,
To look back someday
With contented grin
That, having come thus far
Was worth it all

At end of day, as head hits hay
That we may, self muse to make our peace
And hope, for all our noughts,
Our Maker will be kind enough
And grant us our deserved
Final reprieve

Section 7 :
At Final Goal Post

Seeking Again

Rendezvous Done, Pack Shack, Adieu

Laughed, Cried
Played out work
Worked out play
Lived up strife
Lived through life
Tried it all truly
Well, done, it all

Started it all, with
Crawl, step, climb & fall
Despite yet, standing tall
Ever & always, all clement
No matter the inclement
Hanging up sock,
No lament at all

Tides have now run full froth
Winds & breeze, now chill
Flesh & marrow deep in bone
Keeping step is such a chore

Rather, to reminisce along the shore
Or,
Holding hot broth, some lucky brew
To sit by hearth,
Seeking allies from shadows creeping so

A sudden step, some broken twig
Rasping in tune, to candor tweak
Knocks who now, returned from the ages
Those rogues who departed,
 Or, mayhaps, someone kind in seek?

The Vast Beyond

For, the most who, one time,
Had stood in herald so clear,
Have passed on.
Beyond all realm of near & dear
And those, who drawn
From self-owned toil & toll,
Have flown the coup,
Far beyond, ageing holds of ours & min

With all its run and its fun, Life,
Once, all adventure, now mere overture
Slow reruns of fading frames
As shadows and dark stalk real, retail

And then it sudden came to mind
The "I" was soon to come to end
An abyss that was once mine, so long,
With its still & silence, again in beckon

Soon, all this to be over, bygone
This venture of life, firmly begone
To be free to reach once again,
That firm and peace of the eternal still
So long well known,
And yet, seemingly a void, unknown

The still that was, with all "I" unknown,
True homecoming, on hand,
To be at peace, in deep prayer
Thrilling to be again, in the awaiting
Beyond

With a career span in Corporate Industry of three decades and more, the author has picked up new canvas to put to ink, as in weaning away from the regimen of 12 hrs+ daily work schedules with no respite for anything other than just that….work, work, work, and just more and more work!

Keitiekei is the pen name of the young heart residing in an experienced frame; and, the author & poet within, is of firm opinion that it is indeed high time to dive deep within and dig out the latent and true inner self; to connect with the Universe and world at large, from the landscape of pure heart-speak, more than the rhetoric of the prim and proper overtone of formal rhote of repetitive in communications and speech.

Happy Perusal Folks!
Truly & Forever Yours,
Keitiekei

The Eternal Tug Within